For Mason, my son and future ride buddy,
and for Ryan, my coaster cousin.

R
is for Roller Coaster

An ABC Guide for Future Thrill Seekers

by Aimee Carver

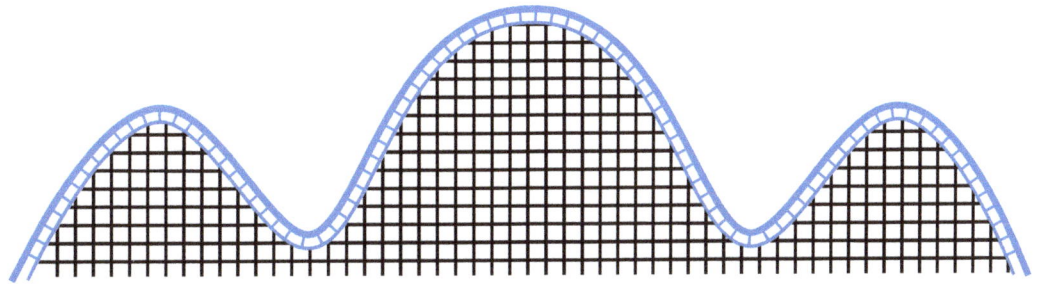

A
is for Airtime

Airtime gives your stomach a tickle and your hair a toss.

A is also for:

Alpine coaster, Axis coaster, Aqua trax coaster, Air launch coaster, Air gates, Anti-rollback device, Ascent, Acceleration, Adrenaline, Amusement park, American Coaster Enthusiasts (ACE), Arrow Dynamics

"IRON RATTLER" AT SIX FLAGS FIESTA TEXAS IN SAN ANTONIO, TEXAS

"SUPERMAN ULTIMATE FLIGHT" AT SIX FLAGS DISCOVERY KINGDOM IN VALLEJO, CALIFORNIA

is for Barrel roll

Barrel rolls twist you tightly around the track.

B is also for:

Bobsled coaster, Boomerang coaster, Banked turn, Bunny hill, Batwing, Bowtie, Butterfly, Banana roll, Backwards, Beyond vertical, Block, Bench seat, Buzz Bar, Brakes, Brake run, Brake fin, Brave, Bolliger & Mabillard (B&M)

C

is for Centripetal force

Centripetal force helps roller coasters travel around an inversion.

C is also for:

Corkscrew, Camelback, Clothoid loop, Cobra roll, Cutback, Compressed air launch, Catapult launch, Centrifugal force, Caisson, Car, Car barn, Chain, Chain lift, Cable lift, Catch brake, Catch car, Capacity, Circuit, Chicken exit, Clone, Credit, Coaster Count, Coaster wars, Cyclone, Coney Island, Chance Rides

"WIPEOUT" AT PLEASUREWOOD HILLS IN LOWESTOFT, ENGLAND

D

is for Dueling coasters

Dueling coasters weave through and around each other, and also sometimes race.

D is also for:

Dark coaster, Double heart coaster, Dive coaster, Dive loop, Dive stall, Dive Drop, Drop, Double loop, Double Dip, Drive tires, Degree, Defunct

is for Exclusive ride time

**Exclusive ride time is
VIP treatment for VIP riders.**

E is also for:

El loco coaster, Euro-fighter coaster, Enclosed coaster, Elevated curve, Elevator cable lift, Electric spiral lift, Electric winch launch, Electromagnetic propulsion, Ejector airtime, Elements, Energy, Enthusiast

"LEVIATHAN" AT CANADA'S WONDERLAND IN VAUGHAN, ONTARIO

"INTIMIDATOR 305" AT KINGS DOMINION IN DOSWELL, VIRGINIA

is for First drop

First drops are always the tallest.

F is also for:

Floorless coaster, Flying coaster, Fourth (4th) dimension coaster, Fourth dimension (4D) Free spin coaster, Family coaster, Free Fly coaster, Figure eight, Flat spin, Fly-to-lie, Forward stall, Friction wheels, Flywheels, Flywheel launch, Free Fall, Floater airtime, Fin brakes, Final brake run

is for Giga coaster

Giga coasters rise between 300-399 feet tall.

G is also for:

Gravity, G-force, Guide wheels, Grab bar, Greyout, Golden ticket, Gift shop, Gerstlauer, Great Coasters International, Gravity Group

"MILLENNIUM FORCE" AT CEDAR POINT IN SANDUSKY, OHIO

"TWISTED COLOSSUS" AT SIX FLAGS MAGIC MOUNTAIN IN VALENCIA, CALIFORNIA

is for Hybrid

Hybrid coasters combine both wood and steel.

H is also for:

Hyper coaster, Hot racer coaster, Hydraulic launch, Heartline roll, Half pipe, Hammerhead, Helix, Hill, Horseshoe, Hangtime stall, Headchopper, Headrest, Harness, Holding brake, High five, Home park

is for Immelmann roll

Immelmann rolls are inversions named after World War I fighter pilot Max Immelmann.

I is also for:

Inverted coaster, Indoor coaster, Impulse coaster, Infinity coaster, Inversion, Inverted top hat, Inclined loop, Inclined dive loop, In-line twist, Interlocking corkscrews, Interlocking loops, Ibox track, Inertia, IAAPA, Intamin

"VALRAVN" AT CEDAR POINT IN SANDUSKY, OHIO

"RUTSCHEBANEN" AT BAKKEN AMUSEMENT PARK IN KLAMPENBORG, DENMARK

is for Jostle

Jostle side to side and up and down in your seat.

J is also for:

Junior coaster, Jr. Immelmann, JoJo roll

is for Kiddie coaster

Kiddie coasters are a great introduction for future thrill-seekers.

"KIDDIE COASTER" AT FUN SPOT AMERICA IN KISSIMMEE, FLORIDA

"BOOMERANG" AT ELITCH GARDENS IN DENVER, COLORADO

is for Loop

Loops are a type of inversion that makes a roller coaster go upside down.

L is also for:

Lightning coaster, Launched coaster, Launch track,
Linear induction motor (LIM), Linear synchronous motor (LSM),
Lateral G-force, Lift hill, Lie-to-fly, Load wheels,
Loading platform, Lap bar, Layout, Line

M

is for Mine train coaster

Mine train coasters typically have a western theme.

M is also for:

Mega coaster, Motorbike coaster, Motocoaster, Multi inversion coaster, Multi dimension coaster, Multi launch coaster, Monorail track, Magnetic brakes, Manufacturer, Mack Rides, Maurer Rides

"SCORPION EXPRESS" AT CHESSINGTON WORLD OF ADVENTURES RESORT IN CHESSINGTON, ENGLAND

"MAKO®" AT SEAWORLD IN ORLANDO, FLORIDA

is for Negative G-force

Negative G-force makes you feel like you're floating.

N is also for:

Negative G-stall loop, Non-inverting loop, Norwegian loop

O

is for Out and back

Out and back roller coasters travel far out after a big drop, then make a u-turn to come back to their station.

O is also for:
Over-the-shoulder restraints (OTSRs), Overbanked turn, Overbanked cutback, On-ride camera, On-ride soundtrack

"GIANT DIPPER" AT BELMONT PARK IN SAN DIEGO, CALIFORNIA

"FURIUS BACO" AT PORTAVENTURA PARK IN SALOU, SPAIN

is for Platform

Platforms are where riders board and exit a roller coaster.

P is also for:

Pipeline coaster, Powered coaster, Powered launch, Pretzel knot, Pretzel loop, Panorama stall, Positive G-force, POV, Pacing, Pneumatics, Physics, Passengers, Philadelphia Toboggan Coasters, Inc., Premier Rides

is for Queue

Queue is another word for line.
Riders must queue up and wait their turn.

ROLLER COASTERS AT SIX FLAGS MAGIC MOUNTAIN IN VALENCIA, CALIFORNIA

R

is for Roller coaster

Roller coasters are amusement park rides with cars on elevated tracks that twist, turn, drop, and sometimes go upside down.

R is also for:

Racing coaster, Reverse free fall coaster, Raptor track, Raven dive, Rising vertical twist, Roll, Reverse cobra Roll, Rollover, Rollback, Road wheels, Restraint, Ride operator, Ride photo, Rider, Re-Ride, Record breaking, Record holder, Rocky Mountain Construction (RMC)

S

is for Strata coaster

Strata coasters tower more than 400 feet into the sky.

S is also for:

Sitting coaster, Stand-up coaster, Shuttle coaster, Suspended coaster, Spinning coaster, Steeplechase coaster, Side friction coaster, Single-rail coaster, Surf rider coaster, Scenic railway, Switchback railway, Sea Serpent, Sidewinder, Spiral lift, Speed hill, Stall, Shoulder harness, Seat, Seatbelt, Skid brakes, Station, Supports, Steel, Steep, Souvenir, Schwarzkopf, S&S – Sensai Technologies

"KINGDA KA" AT SIX FLAGS GREAT ADVENTURE IN JACKSON, NEW JERSEY

"INVERTIGO" AT KINGS ISLAND IN MASON, OHIO

T is for Track

Track is what provides the dips, drops, hills and inversions that make roller coasters so much fun.

T is also for:

Terrain coaster, Triple launch coaster, Tilt coaster, Traveling coaster, Thunderbolt coaster, Twister coaster, Twist and Turn coaster, Topper Track, T-Rex Track, Transfer Track, Tunnel, Top hat, Top Gun stall, Turnaround, Treble clef, Twisted horseshoe roll, Twisting vertical drop, Trick hill, Tester hill, Test seat, Train, Trim brakes, Theming, Theme park, Thrill seeker

is for Underground

Underground tunnels make big drops feel even longer.

U is also for:
Ultra coaster, Unloading platform, Underfriction, Up-stop wheels, Upside down

"VANISH" AT COSMO WORLD IN YOKOHAMA, JAPAN

"THUNDERBOLT" AT LUNA PARK CONEY ISLAND IN BROOKLYN, NEW YORK

is for Vertical drop

Vertical drops send riders straight down.

V is also for:

Virtual reality coaster, Vertical lift coaster, Vertical LSM coaster, Vertical loop, Vertical spiral, Vertical drop track, Valleying, Vekoma

W

is for Woodie

Woodie is a nickname for wooden roller coasters.

W is also for:

Wild mouse coaster, Wing coaster, Water coaster, Wheels, World record

"TROY" AT TOVERLAND
IN SEVENUM, THE NETHERLANDS

"EEJANAIKA" AT FUJI-Q HIGHLAND IN FUJIYOSHIDA, JAPAN

is for X-rail

X-rails help tell 4D roller coasters which way to spin their seats.

X is also for:

Xtreme spinning coaster

is for Yell

Yelling with your hands up makes roller coaster riding so much more fun.

"LEGO® TECHNIC COASTER" AT LEGOLAND IN CARLSBAD, CALIFORNIA

"WICKED" AT LAGOON IN FARMINGTON, UTAH

z

is for Zero-G roll

Zero-G rolls make riders feel weightless as they go upside down while rising and falling.

Z is also for:
Zac spin coaster, Zero-G stall, Zamperla, Zierer

My First Roller Coaster Log

Coaster Name	Park Name	Park Location	Ride Date

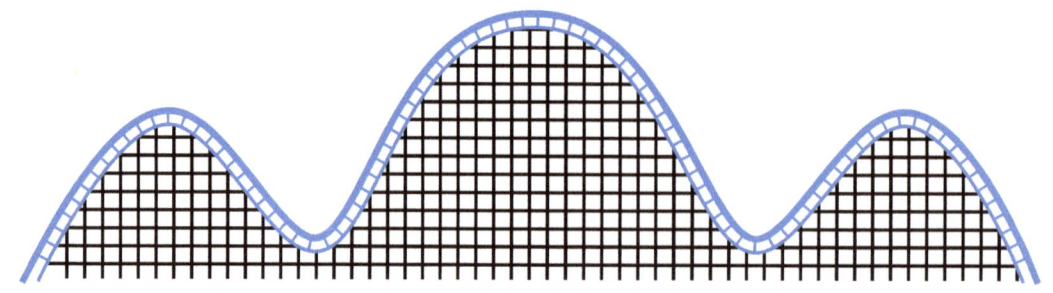

Coaster Name	Park Name	Park Location	Ride Date

Photography Sources

A - Joel A. Rogers - CoasterGallery.com
B - Jeremy Thompson, CC BY 2.0
C - Shutterstock: Martin Charles Hatch
D - Shutterstock: George Sheldon
E - Getty: Randy Risling/Toronto Star
F - Joel A. Rogers - CoasterGallery.com
G - Shutterstock: David McGill 71
H - Shutterstock: Andrea Vassallo
I - Gregory Varnum, CC BY-SA 4.0
J - Shutterstock: Jacob Lund
K - Courtesy of Fun Spot America Kissimmee
L - Shutterstock: Arina P Habich
M - Shutterstock: Lukasz Sadlowski
N - Shutterstock: Viaval Tours
O - Shutterstock: bonandbon
P - Shutterstock: Julien Jean Zayatz
Q - Shutterstock: Shawn Goldberg
R - Shutterstock: Robert V Schwemmer
S - Shutterstock: Marti Bug Catcher
T - Shutterstock: Doug Lemke
U - Shutterstock: MasaPhoto
V - Shutterstock: Elzbieta Sekowska
W - Shutterstock: Arno van Dulmen
X - Shutterstock: ICQ34791919
Y - Shutterstock: Nigel Jarvis
Z - Joel A. Rogers - CoasterGallery.com

About the Author

Aimee Carver rode her first roller coaster when she was five years old, and has been hooked on the rides ever since! She's visited over 50 amusement parks and has hundreds of "coaster credits" to her name. Growing up in New York City, Aimee would take the subway to Coney Island just for a quick Cyclone ride, and she's planned countless road trips and vacations around new roller coaster openings. She now lives in Utah with her husband and their son, whom she's grooming to become her future ride buddy (once he's tall enough!).

 Come along for the ride on Instagram: **@RisforRollerCoaster**

Printed in the USA
CPSIA information can be obtained
at www.ICGtesting.com
LVHW072158031123
762894LV00014B/832